The Parting Glass

By the same author:

Novels

Night Shift
The Woman's Daughter
The Journey Home
Emily's Shoes
A Second Life*
Father's Music
Temptation
The Valparaiso Voyage
The Family on Paradise Pier
New Town Soul*

Collaborative novels

Finbar's Hotel*
Ladies Night at Finbar's Hotel*

Plays

The Lament for Arthur Cleary
Blinded by the Light
In High Germany
The Holy Ground
One Last White Horse
April Bright
The Passion of Jerome
Consenting Adults
From These Green Heights**
The Townlands of Brazil**
Walking the Road*
The Consequences of Lightning**

Poetry

The Habit of Flesh
Finglas Lilies
No Waiting America
Internal Exiles
Leinster Street Ghosts
Taking My Letters back
The Chosen Moment
External Affairs*

Editor

The Picador Book of Contemporary Irish Fiction (UK)
The Vintage Book of Contemporary Irish Fiction (USA)
Night & Day: Twenty Four Hours in the Life of Dublin*

*(*Available from New Island*
***Available from New Island under the title* The Ballymun Trilogy*)*

The Parting Glass

A play

Dermot Bolger

NEW ISLAND

THE PARTING GLASS
First published 2011
By New Island
2 Brookside
Dundrum Road
Dublin 14
Ireland

www.newisland.ie

ISBN: 9781848400917

British Library Cataloguing in Publication Data. A CIP catalogue record for this book is available from the British Library.

Typeset by Arinos Infosolutions.

Cover photograph of Ray Yeates as Eoin by Patrick Redmond, courtesy of axis, Ballymun.

Printed by CPI Anthony Rowe.

New Island received financial assistance from
The Arts Council (An Chomhairle Ealaíon), Dublin, Ireland.

10 9 8 7 6 5 4 3 2 1

Acknowledgements

The Parting Glass was commissioned by **axis** Art Centre, Ballymun, and premiered in **axis**, Ballymun, Dublin, Ireland on June 1st 2010.

Performed by:	Ray Yeates
Directed by:	Mark O' Brien
Set Design:	Robert Ballagh
Lighting Design:	Conleth White
Costume Design:	Marie Tierney
Sound Design:	Mark O' Brien
Producer:	Niamh Ní Chonchubhair
Production Manager:	Dylan Connolly
Stage Manager:	Andrew Campbell
Production Team:	Nicholas Codd, Seán McCormack, Lucy Polden, David Tiernan
Box Office & Marketing:	Philip Keogh

The author would like to thank the actor Ray Yeates, for whom this play was expressly written, and who first played the character of Eoin twenty years ago, in a New York production of the author's initial play about the earlier lives of these same characters, ***In High Germany***.

Introduction

Paula Meehan

Dermot Bolger's new play, a powerful sequel to *In High Germany*, is a journey measured out in soccer matches. Twenty years have passed since Eoin first charmed us with his clear-eyed engagement with exile and the cult of desperation that was the Irish soccer fan's default stance back then. *The Parting Glass* returns him to Ireland with his German wife and son to ride the back of the Tiger. His story is reflected through the life of the national team, his successes and failures map onto their ups and downs, his private life a chorus for the team's life and vice versa. Even if you wouldn't know an offside from a gobstopper, you'll be moved and galvanized by this witness to survival, this marvellous refusal of cynicism. The white-hot passion of a father's love for his son, for his ancestors, for his country, for the beautiful game, for his old pals dead and alive drives this mesmeric and lyrical new work. His grief for his parents, for a simpler life and a life less despoiled is its powerful undersong.

This is a ferocious and disillusioned vision of what it means to be a middle-aged man in modern Ireland, shouldering negative equity, bereavement, redundancy and political betrayal. Its hard-won redemptive wisdom marks this play as a catalyst for hope.

The national team's heart-stopping drama through the late nineties and into this new millennium is the smithy in which one soul's journey through the boom and bust of the Tiger economy is forged. *The Parting Glass* is an unforgettable creation, reminding us that common sense, common decency, loyalty to friends and a willingness to befriend newcomers to Ireland may be the best survival strategy we have. To endure, with compassion and love for self and others, is the message, loud and clear as a bell.

On May 26th, 2010, six nights before the premiere of this play, Bernie Bolger, the beloved wife of its author, collapsed suddenly when swimming with one of their sons and died from an aneurysm. She will always be remembered in the thoughts and prayers of everyone associated with the staging of The Parting Glass.

Blackout. A soundtrack momentarily suggests fragmentary airport announcements. Lights rise on a set consisting of three rows of airport seats: a centre row facing the audience and a row on either side of this, facing into the wings. EOIN, a fifty-year-old man, enters and looks around as if getting his bearings. He wears an old Ireland scarf and carries a shoulder bag. He has a jumper on over an Ireland jersey.

EOIN: *(Distractedly hums)*
Alive-alive-o!
Alive-alive-o!
Stephen Ireland's two grannies
Are alive-alive-o!

Looks at audience.

It was all train stations once: my scenes of homecomings, reunions, destinations reached. Back when

Limerick Junction was the axis of the universe in the arse of nowhere. Astronauts en route to Jupiter used to change trains there, amid fields of lonely-hearted sheep two-timed by love-struck farmers. Asteroids would interrupt thousand-year-long orbits to form orderly queues and blaze past in burnished globes of fire at off-peak times on the Mallow siding. Now it's airports dotted everywhere and a surcharge if you take a deep breath and officials with walkie-talkies larger than apartment blocks in Mountmellick saying: no, you can't take your pen onboard unless you drink the ink first.

When I left Ireland in the 1980s, you had this level of scrutiny, but it wasn't called airport security: it was called suicide watch in Mountjoy Jail. Ryanair still let you bring your shoelaces on board, but only until they figure out how to charge you for the privilege.

The one thing they don't charge you for here in Dublin airport is waiting.

He sits on the centre seats, putting his Ireland scarf in the shoulder bag that he places at his feet. He takes a bottle of water from the bag, and sips from it.

Recovering heroin addicts use this place as a therapeutic half-way house – they can blow the same wad of cash as when addicted: only now they get to spend it on car parking fees. It has cappuccinos and bottled water slightly cheaper than uranium with everyone so busy waiting for something that nobody has time to figure out what I'm waiting here for.

He replaces the bottle in the bag.

The first time I remember waiting for someone I'm six years old and waiting for my Da at Westland Row railway station. Ma has been dolling herself up since dawn so we're like two shiny pins: me in amputated trousers. We reach town early and I'm allowed light a candle in Westland Row Church, though Ma won't say what special intentions she is praying for. But we spend so long amid plastercast saints not noted for conversation that we need to rush into the bustling station. An announcer speaks Swahili in a Cork accent and there, amid the alighting passengers, I see Da coming home with a suitcase in one arm and an overcoat folded in the other.

He rises.

I hold his hand cautiously as we ride the escalator down to the street. I'm nervous of escalators and a bit nervous of him. Da: the absence in my life, the man forced to leave his family to seek work in an English car plant. All my uncles have left and taken their children with them, but Da is stubborn. Da wants me to grow up with an Irish accent under an Irish flag.

Today he's coming home to his wife and son for good: today he ceases to be a weekly registered letter with English banknotes. It's November 1965: Ireland is changing. Men in pubs shout "Hurray for Seán Lemass". But today they also shout for a scrawny Eamon Dunphy making his debut in a green shirt; for John Giles of Leeds and Joe Haverty of Shels, because, for the first time, Ireland is in a playoff against Spain in Paris for a place in the World Cup Finals.

He kneels on the seat, stage right.

The Pearse Street pub is packed with white-shirted men listening to Philip Greene's commentary on the wireless. I'm intoxicated, addicted: living out every kick in my mind. Then, in the eightieth minute, the bar falls silent as Greene announces that Spain has scored. Ma spots my tears.

He rises.

(*Mother's voice*) There'll be other playoffs, son, just you wait and see.

(*Own voice*) She was right: forty-four years on and tonight we were back in Paris for another World Cup playoff. They keep coming around again – just you wait and see. Not that Ma and Da are into waiting – nine months later I have a sister, Maire, with porcelain skin and Mick McCarthy's lungs. I get bribed with a leather football and, out on the street, I win World Cup playoffs for Ireland, scoring late winners with my new best mates. Shane and Mick and me – the three amigos, the bestest best friends forever, just waiting to grow up and play for Ireland.

We wait for girls to cop on that we're sexual studs. We wait for our Leaving Cert results, wait outside Zhivago's nightclub to lose our virginity or even come close to losing our virginity. We wait for our apprenticeships to finish; wait to see Ian Dury and Wreckless Eric play Dublin as unknowns on the Live Stiff Records Tour. We wait for Ireland to qualify for a soccer tournament so we can go there as fans and come home as heroes with stories to tell.

We wait for the evening news so I can see Da picketing outside the American factory that lured him home and shuts down when the tax breaks stop. We wait for Da to accept he'll never find work again; wait for him to die when cancer gets him; wait during the 1980s for someone to give us hope; for Charles Haughey's tax-dodging, criminal cronies to stop screwing us; for soccer referees to stop awarding dodgy decisions against Ireland. We wait for new jobs as, one by one, we lose our old ones. Half of Ireland is waiting in a queue to seek work in McDonald's the day I emigrate in the 1980s to try my luck in Germany. Shane and Mick and me have a drink together in Dublin airport before I leave. This morning we're reunited in another bar – at Charles de Gaulle airport.

He moves forward.

(*As Shane*) How did you get to look so old? Shane asks when his flight lands from Holland.

(*Own voice*) Where do you want me to start, I say, with Mick McCarthy, Roy Keane, Brian Kerr or Steve Staunton? At least I'm in better shape than Mick.

(*As Shane*) Is Mick here?

(*Own voice, holds out an imaginary object*) Say hello to Mick, the compact edition.

He moves back.

(*To audience*) I need to go back four months: a Tuesday morning. My twenty-year-old son Dieter knocks on the bathroom door.

(*As Dieter, German accent*) The post has arrived, Dad, he says. A Jiffy bag from America addressed to you. Maybe it's that box-set I bought on Ebay.

(*Own voice*) Open it, son, I say, I'm shaving.

(*As Dieter*) Dad?

(*Own voice*) Is it the CDs, son?

(*As Dieter*) You know your friend Mick who lives in New York?

(*Own voice*) Mick McKenna, what about him?

(*As Dieter*) He's here.

(*Own voice*) At the door?

(*As Dieter*) In the Jiffy bag.

(*To audience*) I open the bathroom door. Dieter holds an urn. He reads from a card.

(*As Dieter*) "My friend Michael asked me to send you this. Colon cancer is a silent killer, but Michael would never have anything loud. He felt you might find a suitable place to scatter these. He will be sorely missed. Sincerely, L. Perkins."

(*Own voice*) This is a joke, I say, Mick isn't dead. I was just talking to him…

(*As Dieter*) When?

(*Own voice*) I don't know… maybe a year ago or two… I mean the point of old friends is that you don't have to talk to them.

(*As Dieter*) This L. Perkins – whoever he is – doesn't provide a return address. Why send you Mick's ashes?

(*Own voice*) Because Mick's brothers are Neanderthal cavemen who club their own meat in Cabra. Being an illegal immigrant meant he never had to come home and deal with them. Jesus, son, he's younger than me. I can't believe he's dead.

(*As Dieter*) If he wasn't before they cremated him, he certainly is now. What will I do with him, Dad?

(*Own voice*) Stick him in the kitchen.

(*As Dieter*) He'll become a permanent fixture there, and I'm not sure it's hygienic.

(*Own voice*) I'd say they washed him before they burnt him, son.

(*As Dieter*) That's not what I mean.

(*To Dieter*) Put him in the spare bedroom so, I'll deal with him later.

(*As Dieter*) The spare bedroom is where my girlfriend stays.

(*To Dieter*) Dieter, Mick is gay, fifty and cremated: just how safe does a girl need to be? What part of the phrase *I'll deal with him later* do you not understand?

(*As Dieter*) The part that means his ashes will be sitting here in a year's time. Phone your friend Shane in Holland.

(*To Dieter*) I haven't phoned Shane in years. We've nothing in common any more.

(*As Dieter*) You three were inseparable once.

(*To Dieter*) Once is a surprisingly long time ago.

He moves forward.

(*To audience*) All the same I do wind up showing Shane the urn in Charles de Gaulle airport.

(*As Shane*) A surprising amount of ash for a little fellow, Shane says. Is that Mick with the waistcoat or without the waistcoat, would you say? Without, I suspect. They'd have hardy fished out the buttons afterwards.

(*Own voice*) I don't think the buttons would survive the cremation, I say.

(*As Shane*) They survived everything else: you could never get that waistcoat off the little fecker. I miss him badly, you know that.

(*Own voice*) Yeah.

(*As Shane*) Never saw him in years, but I miss him.

(*Own voice*) I know.

(*As Shane*) After you phoned with the news I went to sit in my car in the privacy of the underground car park so nobody would see my crying. I don't know why, I fucking live alone since the divorce. We need a drink, Eoin, for old time's sake. (*Calls*) Bartender, two beers and a water for our mate in the urn, he's a tad dry.

He moves back.

(*To audience*) We put Mick up on the counter between us. He didn't say much but Mick never did. Shane had rarely let him get in a word edgeways. The last time the three of us were together was at the 1988 European Championships in Germany. Ireland had finally qualified for something and we stood, shoulder to shoulder, on the terraces like we had done at Ireland games since we were boys. Sleeping on floors, bumming lifts, scraping together the money to follow our team and coming home like heroes with stories to tell. But no one was going home to Ireland after Euro 88 ended. Home had shifted elsewhere. Shane had found work in Eindhoven. Mick was soon to disappear into the maelstrom of New York as an illegal immigrant, and I stayed on in Germany because I'd a new life there. I'd found love and employment and I had a son about to be born.

Welcome to my Hamburg years. During Italia 90 Dieter cries in his mother Frieda's arms, frightened by the sight of his father kneeling before the television, screaming (*Kneels*): "Jesus, let anyone take the penalty but O'Leary". O'Leary scores, joy is unconfined. (*Rises*) Maiden aunts disrobe in Ballinrobe. God knows what they do in Termonfeckin. Bachelor farmers conduct orgies in horseboxes with livestock whose faces are unfortunate enough to bear a passing resemblance to Mick McCarthy's. In Dublin crowds heave with joy, as delirious as if they'd got to share Liam Lawlor's wealth. And outside our apartment in Hamburg silence reigns, like it is just another day and Ireland haven't reached the quarter finals of the World Cup.

Welcome to happy years – for Irish soccer and for me. Do I miss Ireland? I'm too busy missing sleep. Dieter appears at dawn, demanding cuddles, insisting I accompany him to the kitchen where he draws houses with fantastical designs – houses with wings and wheels – but every house containing matchstick versions of Frieda and me and him in our tiny republic of love. Everything is made new through his eyes. Dieter keeps learning and so do I: night courses in new technologies for a new Germany, a new Europe without borders. Countries reborn through plebiscites and uncivil wars; walls collapsing, old hatreds enflamed, tanks and treaties and families reunited.

I have learnt my father's lesson: you should never return, but I can't fully let go of Ireland though. In dreams I'm still here and every time they play soccer I find a television. Those eleven men in green – twinning the accents from the sons of those who stayed and those forced to leave – feel like the only Ireland I still belong to.

On visits home my untouched bedroom is a mausoleum to me. My dead father's presence pervades the house where my mother lives for Bingo and loves to watch wrestling on television. Water is splashed so often on Dieter's head behind our backs that he becomes the most baptized tourist in Ireland.

It breaks my heart that this is all he is in Ireland: a tourist surveying his father's past. He is six when Ireland beat Italy one nil in the 1994 World Cup in America. He races around our apartment cheering while Frieda laughs at our antics. In Eindhoven Shane sits in his car in an underground car park to emit an uninterrupted scream of joy that won't waken his baby daughter. Shane who has been reconstructed by his Dutch wife: whose teeth are fixed; who has acquired glasses once worn by a Czechoslovakian dissident, who dresses like a Jesuit into light bondage and vaguely smells of baby vomit.

But Mick is actually present in New York to witness that famous Irish victory. He walks tall from the Giants Stadium. He is still walking tall that night when he steps from a gay sauna in the Meatpackers district and is kicked to within an inch of his life by three Puerto Ricans.

A random encounter, a fluke, like Ray Haughton's goal in the Giants Stadium itself. What do you do when you've been beaten up but you don't officially exist? Do you go to the police? Risk betraying your identity in hospital as an illegal alien? Or limp home and patch yourself up? Who can you tell when your two best mates don't know you're gay; when your brothers don't know, when your mother knows but doesn't say, when you exist in two worlds and barely say a word in either.

Mick sends funny postcards to Dieter and phones once a year after some dire Irish match. "Jesus wept" – the bible's shortest sentence, an epic communiqué from him after Macedonia broke our hearts, when we came within seconds of qualifying for the World Cup again.

The three amigos in three different worlds. Each time Ireland plays, Mick sits in the Red Lion pub in Manhattan's Bleecker Street, among exiled fans shouting at pictures from Lansdowne Road. In Hamburg, I'm in the Shamrock Bar in Feldstrasse. In Eindhoven, Shane sits in O'Shea's pub on Jan van Lieshoutstraat. The 1990s roll on – the Irish economy soars and Irish football collapses. We enter playoff limbo, beaten first by the Dutch and then by Belgium in 97 when Dieter is nine years old. He's silently crying and he's only set foot in Ireland four times – admittedly, three times more than some Irish internationals. I feel like a torchbearer, with football being his only link to Ireland until one day in the park he says:

(*Dieter's accent*) Dad, can we please stop playing football? I don't like it.

(*Own voice*) We do everything else together, his hand inseparably in mine: on the street, on the U-bahn, on weekend walks by the jetties of Blankenese. Frieda nicknames us: E.D., Eoin and Dieter.

(*Frieda's accent*) It's good we didn't call him Thomas, she teases – E.T. would be too much to live with, always wanting to go home.

(*Own accent*) But that's what I secretly yearn to do when I see Dieter caught up in German cartoons and crazes, worlds I can't fully enter.

He moves forward.

(*As Shane*) Mick and his hidden worlds, eh, Shane says in the bar at Charles de Gaulle. I thought I knew him so well, yet I might never have known he was gay had I not said to him on the phone – the time Ireland lost our third fucking playoff in a row, to Turkey "at least we're not gay or Rovers fans". "Well, seeing as you've finally brought up the subject," he says.

(*Own accent*) Had you a problem with it? I ask.

(*Shane's voice*) None, though he could have said he was in the wardrobe before we shared a sleeping bag in the communal tent at the Lisdoonvarna festival.

(*Own accent*) I think you mean "in the closet", I say.

(*Shane's voice*) I grew up next door to him and the McKennas were lucky to have wardrobes, never mind closets. There was no fear of him being a transvestite anyway – any McKenna would be too mean to fork out for the clobber. I sometimes go back over the jokes we used to make as kids. Not that we were biased against gays, mind you...

(*Own voice*) No, I say, before we left Ireland we were biased against everybody.

(*Shane's accent*) I fucking hate them, Shane says then. I fucking hate them.

(*Own voice*) Who? Gay people?

(*Shane's accent*) Don't be daft. Being gay in Holland is as posh as being a Kildare Protestant. It's fucking Irish people I've come to hate: smug bastards visiting Holland, dripping hints of wealth like an old dog drips piss. I'm glad Ireland is bankrupt. I got sick of pitying looks when they discovered I emigrated in the 1980s, like I was the biggest spa on earth, the gobshite who stopped feeding the one-armed bandit moments before it hit the jackpot.

(*Own voice*) You still came here to Paris for the playoff when Dieter got us tickets, I say. You'll still roar your head off tonight.

(*As Shane*) Soccer is different, Shane says. Following Ireland is an incurable affliction, like baldness or premature ejaculation: you just can't help yourself. Besides I hate the Dutch more. I've spent twenty years wading through cotton wool, with neighbours so reasonable you want to shoot them. I've become like them in so many ways. I bore myself as a Dutchman when I'm not boring people as a Paddy in O'Shea's Bar. I keep criticizing Ireland and biting the head off anyone else who dares to. I don't even recognize Ireland any more since it became every multinational's favourite rogue state, since it got sucked into the biggest pyramid selling scam in history. I mean, Eoin, what the fuck possessed you to go home?

(*To audience*) What possessed me? You can build new life abroad, but you're never free of a place while you have a parent alive. Ma alone in that house where I was born, slowly going daft. She is wandering the streets at three a.m. when struck by a truck. The panicked phone call from my sister that every emigrant dreads. Cheap flights home are not cheap when you're in a hurry. But at least I can go home, unlike Mick trapped in New York. Ma pulls through.

He moves to seats, stage left.

I find her sitting bolt upright in bed in the Mater hospital like a bus passenger desperate not to miss her stop. Ribs broken, face bruised, lips stitched up, but interested only in getting home.

He sits.

Ma, do you know who I am?

(*As Mother*) Didn't I marry you? She says. I know what's happening: even if that daughter of yours keeps trying to confuse me. She tricked me in here.

(*Own voice*) Maire is my sister, Ma. She's trying to mind you.

(*As Mother*) You don't have an Irish face at all. But all you nurses are foreign.

(*To audience*) I meet Maire in the corridor. She looks exhausted.

He rises.

(As Maire) Ma just sits at home curled up in a ball of fear, Maire says.

(*Own voice*) I phone her most days from Hamburg, I say. I send photos of Dieter.

(As Maire) That's still not doing your share, you're not being scolded and summoned every day.

(Own voice) That's not my fault.

(As Maire) Nobody forced you to leave. People were always saying, poor Eoin, the emigrant, but you got away scot-free.

(Own voice) That's not fair.

(As Maire) I know. Maire grips my hand. But life isn't fair when I'm left here dealing with this shit and you're not. I miss having you around, Eoin. Ireland is brimming with people, but I barely know my own neighbours now.

(*Own voice*) How's Theo, I ask, remembering the little gobshite Shane and Mick and me were forced to bring playing pitch and putt when he started dating my teenage sister and fancied himself as Ballybough's answer to Severiano Ballesteros.

(*As Maire*) Theo's good with money. He's having an affair with his pocket calculator. One morning I woke up to discover that all my neighbours are Polish and my husband had become an American.

(Own voice) I'm here for you now, I say.

(*As Maire*) Let's be honest, Eoin, you're not.

(*To audience*) Ma insists on going home. The hospital thrilled because, although Ireland is suddenly rich, we still have an eighteen month wait for nursing homes.

He moves behind the centre row of seats.

I fly back to Hamburg but I'm only half there. Frieda finds me standing alone on the balcony at two a.m.

(*Frieda's accent*) Not being at home for your mother is tearing you in two, she says.

(*Own voice*) That was always part of the price of a new life in Hamburg.

(*As Frieda*) When we first met, Frieda says, you talked about earning enough money to go home. I used to feel I trapped you in Germany.

(*Own voice*) You're my only true home now, I say, you and Dieter. Wherever you are, I belong.

(*As Frieda*) My company are opening a hub in Kildare, she says. They're offering two-year contracts to experienced line managers.

(*Own voice*) We're settled in Hamburg.

He sits.

(*Frieda's voice*) People change, countries change, marriages change.

(*Own voice*) Are we changing, Frieda?

(*Frieda's voice*) Maybe we're too settled.

(*Own voice*) I'm scared to make the same mistake as my dad, I say, scared of believing in Ireland and having my hopes dashed.

(*Frieda's voice*) Your father was man enough to emigrate and man enough to return. You were willing to stay here for me; I'm willing to go there for you. When we first met you made me laugh. You shook up my world and had terrible taste in underwear. Maybe we need to shake up our world again.

(*To audience as he stands*) Maybe we do. For years Ireland has been an unresolved phantom pain inside me. Suddenly Dublin is Europe's trendiest capital, Ireland's economic miracle proclaimed in every business supplement. As a child I stood outside Trinity

College in Dublin, afraid to go in. I realise that what I want most is for my father's ghost to see Dieter enter an Irish university by right and know that we kowtow to nobody any more. Dieter will never have an Irish accent, but he can still get a sense of where he sprang from. Dieter doesn't do teenage histrionics, he is cool about giving Ireland a try.

(*To Dieter*) What about your friends, I say.

(*As Dieter*) It's called Facebook, Dad.

(*To Audience*) On our last night in Hamburg I watch Frieda get ready for bed.

(*To Frieda*) Are things changing between us? I ask.

(*Frieda's accent*) I'm ready for a change, Eoin. Seduce me. Show me someone I don't know.

He moves to the seats, stage right.

(*To audience*) Suddenly I know I'm not going home for my mother: I'm going home for myself. I'm calling my own bluff, claiming my inheritance in a new land of tall skinny lattes and gleaming apartment blocks. I'm going home to fulfil my father's dreams. Dublin airport is a massive building site the morning we fly home. The route in from the airport is the same: cranes and earthmovers – a pandemic of SUVs. All the women have turned blonde, all the waitresses speak Latvian. The bookies in Dorset Street are now sex shops. The girls buying John Player Blue at Hardwick Street flats are so posh they have a different pair of pyjamas to wear to the shops every day.

Dublin is so dear we wind up renting on a vast estate in Leixlip. I have a job arranged within days and two better offers before I sign the contract. I get lost on new roads driving to see my mother. Some mornings I feel an exhilarated sense of belonging. On other mornings I feel more of an immigrant than Frieda. And so a year passes in a cocoon of work and sleep and endless traffic tailbacks. Ireland is a jigsaw under construction. It is Polish shops and Romanian bodybuilders and African mothers outside schools. It is unexpected estates dropped from space. It is Sunday walks with Frieda on Howth Head to show her pubs I remember and find places I don't. Seduce me, show me someone I don't know. I push the bedroom door softly closed while Dieter chats on Facebook to old friends in Germany and new friends from the German school in Clonskeagh. I kiss Frieda's lips in the dark. I know I have taken the risk of coming home and I am blessed.

He moves forward.

(*As Shane*) So, was it love? Shane asks while the bar in Clarles de Gaulle fills with Irish fans with tricolours and Leprechaun hats the size of Fionn mac Cumhaill's codpiece.

(*Own voice*) Was what love?

(*To Shane*) Mick and the mysterious L. Perkins.

(*Own voice*) You tell me, I say. You knew Mick better than anyone.

(*As Shane*) I thought I knew him. But for the second half on my life – the half lived abroad – I didn't know him at all. I'd phone him and we'd talk shite about soccer. It was our way of acknowledging that we'd nothing else to talk about now. I always got a great kick when he phoned and a sense of relief when he'd hang up. You always get a great kick if anyone phones when you live alone.

(*Own voice*) Surely you have friends in Holland? I say.

(*As Shane*) We had gansey-loads of friends, Shane says. "We" being the important word. Couples, couples and more couples. I was the life and soul of every dinner party, soirée and Bar Mitzvah. Folks found my jokes funny, but then I realised that they found everything I said funny. I was so funny that one day I stopped being funny because it wasn't funny anymore.

(*Own voice*) What made you split up? I ask.

(*As Shane*) Irreconcilable differences: I was different and my wife was irreconcilable. I'm alone, but maybe essentially we're always alone or waiting to be alone. You outgrow friendships and marriages and nationalities and one day you find that life is like a pint of milk: it's no one's fault that it's just gone sour. You fight with your wife for years and it's bitter and intense, but that's because she's so much a part of you that you're really fighting with yourself. No war is more uncivil than a civil war. Tooth and nail and not an inch and then six and a half inches – or in my case, nine and a half – because the fighting is just another form of foreplay. Then one day it's not foreplay; it's things that can't be unsaid. You grow accustomed to the feel of a body in bed beside you, Shane says, and one day it's gone.

(*To audience*) In that first year in Leixlip Frieda is my alarm clock. I wake beside her and I know it's three a.m. and my bladder is betraying my age. At half four I wake again to the warmth of her skin inches away that I dare not cross and disturb her when we're due hot dates with traffic jams. But I luxuriate in her aroma that oozes sex and smells vaguely Lutheran. I ponder the nape of her neck, the curve of her buttocks. Eighteen years since we first slept together and I'm still wonderstruck at her body in the moonlight.

He moves back.

I long for her to wake and turn, with her old gaze of exasperation and longing. Where are our lives going, I want to ask her, in this estate of a thousand identikit houses; this orgy of cul-de-sacs in the mayhem of Kildare; this scurry of ants racing at dawn to the motorway, the crèche, the designated parking space.

He sits.

Frieda can handle the Irish weather – she calls it permanent October: good October and bad October. But Irish traffic defies her logic. Therefore when I wake at half five I find only the aftertrace of her warmth in the bed. I hear the shower and want to clamber in with her – like in the early Hamburg years – for fully exhilarating dawn sex, after which I always felt so alive, walking to the bakery for hot Müsli-Brötchen crammed with raisins.

In Leixlip it takes military planning just to drive to the garage and buy a breakfast roll. So I fall back asleep, knowing I need to drop Dieter off at school before rat-racing to work. My mobile phone beside the bed wakes me. Frieda is approaching the steep bridge at Sallins. She wants me to check if she has taken out meat to defrost from the freezer. I try to say something witty but there's a moratorium on wit at dawn. Then Frieda says softly: "This is pure crazy".

What is crazy – the traffic, our lives together? Were we pure crazy to move from Hamburg? Before I can ask there is a bang so close it might be in the bedroom. I think I hear her gasp, but how could I hear a gasp over the noise of imploding metal, the glass shards cascading from the windscreen? The silence that follows is so deep it's like the world is afraid to breathe. Nothing could survive the impact, but her phone does, only it seems to come from a long way away. I hear car doors open, a voice saying "Sweet Christ". Then her phone dies as if giving up the ghost, unable to cling on.

He stands.

I need to wake Dieter but I'm afraid to wake Dieter. I run to my car, but not to rescue her; I'm running away from the need to comfort my son. I need Frieda to be alive so I can ask her what to do. Please God, don't take her from me. I mount kerbs and break red lights, speed in the bus lane. When I reach the tailback I abandon my car. I run through stalled lines of cars towards flickering ambulance lights. Never have I run so fast and never has time moved so slow. Then I crest the cordoned-off tape and confront the three construction workers who ploughed into her. Their upturned car faces the wrong way. Trapped inside, they stare unblinkingly out, puzzled by how they got here.

They remind me of Shane and Mick and me at twenty-one, when life was a permanent buzz and we were always broke and out for fun. Were they joking in Polish about the cowboy who sold them this heap of junk? No tax, no insurance, no NCT. This is pure crazy, Frieda's last words, watching them speed towards her on the wrong side of the road.

Frieda's car doesn't resemble a car. The police won't let me through. It has a gold sticker, I say, so we can tell her phone apart from Dieter's. Nobody listens until a policewoman walks up the cordoned off road, gingerly holding a mobile phone with a gold star. They lift back the blanket for a half-second to let me see if Frieda is there. Frieda's gone.

He kneels.

(*Paramedic's voice*) We thought she was foreign too, a paramedic says. Those East Europeans drive like it's 1981.

(*Own voice*) She is foreign, I say. I'm foreign here too. I'm lost.

(*Paramedic's voice*) Maybe you should ride in the ambulance, sir.

(*Own voice*) I was thinking I might hold her hand.

(*Second paramedic's voice*) You do that.

(*Own voice*) Frieda's fingers are cold. I touch the ring I bought her as a surprise in a jewellers shop in Wellingsbüttel on Dieter's first birthday.

(*Frieda's voice*) Is this a proposal? Frieda asks.

(*Own voice*) Only if you want it to be.

(*Frieda's voice*) There's only one way for you to find out.

(*Own voice*) Meine Liebe und mein Leben, will you take this love-struck, clodhopper Irishman to be your husband, because he is daft about you and you're the only country he now belongs to.

(*Frieda's voice*) What is a clodhopper?

(*Own voice*) Like a grasshopper, with hobnail boots and a Mayo accent. Frieda, marry me. I love you. I'd be lost if you ever left me.

(*Frieda's voice, amused*) Why would I ever leave you?

(*Own voice*) All this time I'm talking to her the paramedics are saying nothing, because what can you say to a man proposing marriage to a corpse? In Leixlip Dieter is waking up in an empty house. I need to be strong for him but I'm not strong. I'm a foreigner hurling at such speed through traffic that I no longer know where I am.

He rises and steps back.

(*As Dieter, softly*) Vater? (*No reply*) Dad?

(*Own voice*) What do you want, Dieter?

(*As Dieter, softly*) I want you to go to bed. It's nearly dawn.

(*Own voice*) I'm not sleepy, son.

(*As Dieter*) I miss Mutti too, every second of every day.

(*Own voice*) You're my whole world now, Dieter, my heart and soul. I'm so immensely proud of you.

(*As Dieter*) What's there to be proud of? I've done nothing.

(*Own voice*) It's not what you've done, it's who you are.

(*As Dieter*) I'm just myself.

(*Own voice*) That's a miracle few people achieve.

(*To audience*) I don't recall Da praising me like that, or praising me at all. A generation of subterfuge and camouflage who never expressed emotion: drifting icebergs of men with only the barest tip showing. That's what I feel myself becoming – a silent provider working on autopilot. My line supervisor says I don't need to work so hard but I want to live suspended in a limbo of priority consignments of computer parts, with credit details being checked in New Delhi call centres. I would work twenty-four hours a day were it not for Dieter. No, I tell a lie. I would hang myself.

(*Frieda's voice*) "Hang yourself?" I imagine Frieda's voice. "You couldn't even hang up a washing line for me."

He moves to seats, stage right.

(*Own voice*) I don't just imagine Frieda's voice; at night I listen to her telephone answering message that I can't bring myself to delete.

(*Frieda's voice*) I cannot take your call just now because all that remains of me is a wardrobe crammed with blouses; a dressing table awash with jewellery; anti-ageing creams; a jar of moisturiser with my fingerprint still visible in it.

(*Own voice*) Her must-do list to herself that I come home one day to find gone. (*Annoyed*) Dieter, where are your mother's clothes?

(*Dieter's voice*) Gone.

(*Own voice*) What do you mean, gone?

(*Dieter's voice*) I gave them to the charity shop on Main Street: it took me seven trips with seven black plastic sacks. At first the women got cross that Mutti was sending down too much. Then they realised I was packing it myself. They say they will display nothing in the window in case it upsets me when I pass.

(*Own voice*) You had no right, Dieter.

(*Dieter's voice*) One of us had to deal with this and it was never going to be you.

(*To audience*) No fifteen-year-old boy should have to carry his mother's life away in seven plastic sacks. Dieter goes to do his homework and I sit shivering in Frieda's old bedroom, with the window wide open until every trace of her scent is gone. Then I put on a clean shirt and tell Dieter not to stay up. I'm going out to meet a woman. I'm going to get drunk and talk shite for Ireland and do whatever it takes it break this spell of grief. Only I don't go drinking. I wait at the bus stop for town, huddled against the wind, letting bus after bus pass, as I stare across at that charity shop. Then, when it grows late enough, I walk home and rattle around the bathroom for Dieter's sake, as if I've enjoyed a carefree evening, like I'm a bachelor now happily facing into a new life.

He sits on the centre seat for a moment to take a sip from the bottled water in his bag. There is no interval but this slight pause marks the play's halfway point. He rises and steps forward.

EOIN: We're on our second pint at Charles de Gaulle when Dieter joins us. He's been making his own arrangements.

(*As Shane*) Give us a look at you, Shane says. You have it all, boy – looks, intelligence, charm, charisma. It's natural, of course, these qualities always skip a generation.

(*As Dieter*) You haven't changed, Dieter says.

(*As Shane*) No, I'm still talking shite in some bar. Thanks for the match ticket. I hope they didn't break the bank.

(*Own voice*) He broke his girlfriend's heart, I say. Her Da works for the FAI. He only told her his news after she got him three tickets to the playoff.

(*As Shane*) Good luck, kid. It can be a tough road. For once I know what I'm talking about. Listen, I worry that I might be intruding on a family occasion here? Three can be a crowd.

(*Own voice*) We're four. I pick up the urn. Four is a standard defensive formation.

(*As Shane*) We're a fairly standard Irish back four alright, Shane replies; two of us are over the hill, one has a foreign accent and one is dead. Mick is doing well: New York to Dublin for a price of a postage stamp, then Dublin to Paris in someone's pocket and he's going to get into his final Ireland match for nothing. For a man disinclined to spend money, this may be as close to heaven as it gets. Have you figured out where we scatter the ashes?

(*Own voice*) After the match I was thinking of the Champs-Élysées, I say.

(*As Shane*) A back lane in Pigalle might be more Mick's style.

(*As Dieter*) Choose wherever you like, Dieter says, but let's not make this a wake. I see this more as a celebration of what's gone and the chance for a fresh start.

(*As Shane*) Ireland in a playoff? Trust me, Shane says, it will be a fecking wake.

(*To Audience*) Six months after Frieda's death Dieter and I try to make a fresh start. I offer to return to Hamburg but Dieter says that Hamburg holds too many memories for us both. We leave our rented house amid the cul-de-sacs of Leixlip. Renting is for Asians and Eastern European carpenters with shaved heads. My brother-in-law badgers me into seeing my bank manager and my bank manager laughs when I query if I can really afford to borrow all he suggests. Borrow what it takes, the bank manager says; just get a foot on the property ladder before it's whipped up. He makes me sound like the last monk stranded outside a round tower before the Vikings arrive.

I want somewhere with no echoes of Frieda. I want mortgage sub-clauses to focus on because nothing feels real, everything filtered through a dull ache. We buy in Inchicore: a third storey apartment that looks great in a brochure. It has the kind of underground car park where the mafia shoot people in films.

Three months later I get an unexpected cheque: Frieda's company had a staff insurance policy I knew nothing about. Suddenly Dieter's future is as bright as Ireland's: he will have money to do whatever he wishes. I want him to stay here. I want grandchildren with Irish accents. I have my dead father's dreams and my brother-in-law's hectoring advice when Theo insists on treating me to a round of golf in the K Club.

(*As Theo*) I promised Maire to get you out of yourself, he says on the first tee. What will you do with the insurance money?

(*Own Voice*) I'll put half on deposit for Dieter, I say. I'll pay off some of my mortgage with the rest. I owe the bank a small fortune.

(*As Theo*) We're all meant to owe the banks a small fortune, Theo says; otherwise they wouldn't be worth a big fortune. Pay off nothing and put nothing on deposit: invest every cent.

(*Own voice*) Tee off, Theo, I say; the fourball is out of range.

(*As Theo, mimes a practice swing*) Not with this Big Bertha, they're not. This driver is Titanium forged with Viagra. It's as good as sex... or sex with your sister – sorry, no offence.

(*Own voice*) Just tee off, Theo.

(*As Theo)* Your problem, Eoin, is that you were abroad for too long. Irish history only properly began a decade ago when we stopped being scared of our own shadows, when we stopped leaving money on deposit or under mattresses and started to take risks. You missed the boat by buggering off to Germany, now don't miss it twice. There's no one as poor as a returned yank. If you'd had the balls to scrape together the deposit on a house twenty years ago, your investment would have grown by two thousand percent.

(*Own voice*) Did you ever consider setting up as a grief councillor, Theo? I say. You've all the attributes.

(*As Theo*) I also have four houses in flats. Some nice Filipina nurses as tenants if you're lonely for female company...

(*Own voice*) Hit the ball, Theo, or hit me but just shut up.

(*As Theo, miming playing a golf shot*) There's no point being a monk unless you're an inner city criminal. (*Calls*) Fore!

(*Own voice, mimes watching the ball*) You're insensitive and a hooker.

(*As Theo)* It takes balls of steel to drive a Titleist Pro V1 so far out of bounds. *(Looks up)* If you want Dieter to survive here don't let his inheritance gather dust. I don't mean go crazy and invest it in the sort of Soviet satellites where the Provos launder their cash. Play it safe – Anglo Irish bank shares: the best run bank on earth. Sean Fitzpatrick has done more for Ireland than Pearse ever did. Sure, anywhere where a tight arsed Fermanagh fecker like Sean Quinn stacks his shekels is good enough for me. We're talking about Dieter's future. If he wants to be able to buy a house in five years time then money left on deposit will be about as useful as Bohemians Football Club in Europe. (*Mildly hurt*) And I'm not insensitive: I'm a new man. Maire says I can even get my tongue around corners. Now, get up on that tee box. Hold this driver like she was your girlfriend and hit it like she was your wife.

(To audience) I invest every cent. It seems easier than being forced to play golf with him again. I invest in blue-chip Irish bank shares

to show I'm a responsible parent. Theo says to think in terms of five to ten years. I can't even think in terms of five to ten days: I focus on getting through each night, aching for Frieda. I need someone to put their arms around me, but I can't burden Dieter any further. I must break this spell of grief. You're a single man now, Eoin, I tell myself. How often does every married man wish to go back out on the pull? You can do this: you're not a tongue-tied fifteen-year-old any more.

Steps forward, looks around.

Then why do I feel a palpable terror, walking into Café en Seine in Dawson Street on a Friday night? I'm more scared than if about to perform open-heart surgery. Chattering faces throng the bar. How long since I chatted up a girl? Back when the Vikings fled Dublin for fear of having their longboats clamped. (*He moves back*) I order a drink for Dutch courage, then one for German courage. There are twenty-seven European Union member states – when I reach Slovenian courage I'll be rightly scuttered. There's such a wall of sound it's like being inside a Phil Spector record. I go to leave but it's virtually impossible to reach the door. The bar is packed like a lifeboat on the Titanic, women and merchant bankers first. I wind up trapped beside a woman also trying to escape. Her breasts press into my shirt. In order not to stare at them I'm stare at her face, the situation so absurd we're both smiling as we push our way out onto Dawson Street.

He moves quickly forward.

(*Woman's voice*) That's the last time I'll try and meet someone in there, she says. I mean "meet someone" as in meet the girls from work.

(*Own voice*) I know, I say, I was meeting two mates, Shane and Mick.

(*Woman's voice*) Were they inside?

(*Own voice*) No. They had a long way to come.

(*Woman's voice, awkwardly*) Goodnight, she says.

(*Own voice*) Eh… seeing as your friends didn't show, I say, I mean if you're free...

(*Woman's voice*) I'm not free, she says, nothing is ever free.

(*Own voice*) Give me a break, I say. I'm rusty and was never good at this. How do you ask a woman would she like to go for a drink with you?

(*Woman's voice*) I have to go. I hope your friends surface.

(*Own voice*) One lives in New York, I say, and the other in Eindhoven. I'm a poor liar.

(*Woman's voice*) I like a man who knows what he's poor at. Mine is a brandy and ginger. Make me laugh and I might buy you one back.

He moves to seats, stage right.

(*To audience*) Her apartment is in the Financial Services Centre. Furniture so minimalist it is barely there. She is calm, I'm nervous. She likes it this way.

(*Woman's voice*) Are you married, she asks?

(*Own voice*) I was.

(*Woman's voice*) Separated?

(*Own voice*) We are now.

(*To audience*) I can hear Frieda's impatient whisper in my head: just kiss her. She is studying me. We've met before somewhere, decades ago, maybe at a bedsit party sharing dope and rice crispy buns while people danced and we laughed about the incredible notion of one day being twenty-five.

He sits.

(*Woman's voice*) The forties are the new thirties, she says. Separated is the new single. You are separated, aren't you?

(*Own voice*) I only have a son waiting for me.

(*Woman's voice*) Let's not talk about children. Let's have one night when we've failed at nothing. I'm a success: look around you, we're all successes. We're so successful we should licence the franchise to be Irish. Do you want coffee, Eoin?

(*Own voice*) I think so.

(*To audience*) She disappears into the kitchen and I sit there, wanting to leave and wanting to stay. (*He stands*) When she reappears, she is holding a coffee cup, with a spoon balanced on one side of the saucer and a condom on the other. She is naked.

(*Woman's voice*) Promise me one thing, she says. Promise you won't find your way back here like a wounded dog.

(*To audience*) I don't wake her at four a.m., though I know she's awake. I never get to know her except in the biblical sense and at forty-eight you don't know people in the biblical sense for as long as you once did. I walk home through streets filling with migrant workers and I want to feel Frieda's spirit close to me. But all I feel is alone and satisfied. Dieter's bedroom door is ajar. I stand for a moment to watch him sleep and when I turn his voice surprises me: (*as Dieter*) Mutti would be pleased. (*Own voice*) I sleep like I haven't slept since Frieda's death. When I wake neither of us talk about it again.

He moves back to centre stage.

(*To audience*) It's three o'clock when Shane and Dieter and me reach the centre of Paris. Five thousand Irish fans are singing as they besiege the Eiffel Tower.

(*As Shane*) They're so happy they look like the queue outside the dole office when it's Christmas bonus week, Shane says.

(*To Audience*) To freak out the French cops, someone has the idea that we'll all sit on the ground in silence for ten seconds, then jump up again.

(*As Shane*) The novelty wears off the fifth time you do this, says Shane, scrambling up, a bit like scuba diving or adultery.

(*To audience*) The fans decide to launch into a rendition of La Marseillaise.

(*As Dieter*) It's wonderful, Dieter says. You Irish can now sing two anthems you don't know any of the words of.

(*As Shane*) Fuck off, Shane says. Every Irish person here knows the first three words of Amhran Na bhFiann.

(*Own voice*) And the last three, I say.

(*As Shane*) The bit in the middle is boring anyway. Here, give us that fecking urn.

He kneels.

(*To audience*) Shane sprinkles a small handful of ash onto the concourse.

(*As Shane*) I miss you, you bollix, he says softly. I miss you real bad, pal. He looks up. We'll bring Mick to the match all right, he says. I just thought I'd leave his waistcoat here.

He stands.

(To audience) I had half a mind to buy myself a waistcoat, for my forty-eighth birthday. I always wanted one as a kid.

(*As Dieter)* What else did you always want back then? Dieter asks in our Inchicore apartment.

(*Own voice*) A motorbike.

(*As Dieter*) Buy one, Dad.

(*Own voice*) Don't be daft.

(*As Dieter*) Go for it.

(*To audience*) In the motorbike shop the sales assistant asks if I've ridden a motorbike before.

(*Own voice*) Of course, I say... though it was a moped actually. A girlfriend from Leitrim had one. I think she stole the engine from a lawnmower. I used to ride it when she wasn't looking.

(Biker's accent) God knows what she was riding when you weren't looking, he says. C'mon you'll be grand on this one. With the right helmet, the post-mistress won't know if you've come to rob her or collect your pension.

He sits up on the back of the centre stage seats.

(To Audience) Ten expensive lessons later, Dieter holds onto me as I nose out into Sunday traffic. I steer like my life depends on it because something more precious does: the thing that roots me to this earth, my son who came home with me at a terrible cost, my son who will make sense of history. Before he outgrows me we're bound by the engine's roar, the exhilaration of the breeze sweeping past, the heightened sense of life. At Brittas Bay we see mobile homes the size of Russian penitentiaries: all fur coat and no foundations – fake tans and real tans and men discussing Baltic investment properties and acres of tax incentive holiday homes infesting seaside towns like acne. The woman from Cafe en Seine was right: we Irish are so successful we should franchise ourselves. And one Sunday we drive over the steep bridge at Sallins, saying nothing but knowing we have passed on.

He moves forward.

Dieter switches schools to the Institute in Leeson Street. It's like the Gaeltacht made easy – all the French kissing with none of the irregular Irish verbs. He acquires a Leaving Cert brimming with points and a girlfriend brimming with hormones and decides to study architecture. Well, why not? If anywhere needs architects it's Ireland. Life is so good that God sends us Steve Staunton. Soccer comes to Croke Park but Stephen Ireland can't play because he's attending his granny's Month's Mind.

Then one Tuesday in work we're all brought into the canteen and told we're laid off. It's ridiculous, a Stone Age concept: laid off. Not that the company uses this term from my father's time. They talk of a reorganisation of resources, a concentration of jobs in a new hub in Latvia. In the car park news crews appear.

A girl cries as she talks about her 100% mortgage but it feels like she is crying because she's expected to. It doesn't feel real. This is Ireland in 2007: we're so successful we could franchise ourselves; we're so successful our bankers ejaculate in gold dust. In my car I look at the statutory redundancy figures I've jotted down.

He moves to seats, stage right.

They will only feel real when I sit down with Frieda to discuss them. I start the engine, then turn it off. How – for even a second in shock – could I let myself forget that Frieda is dead?

Theo wants me to invest my statutory redundancy in more Anglo Irish shares. Their price keeps plummeting, based on false rumours, he says. I should snap them up with balls of steel while the blind mice flee. I ignore Theo. I'm too busy watching the money I invested for Dieter's future disappear as Irish shares keep tumbling. Do I ride the market or cut my losses? I don't know what to do. I'm filling in job application forms and not even getting replies. I'm checking the stock market every half hour, trying to stop calculating how much we've lost. I'm not sleeping: the walls of the apartment growing in on me. I'm in a limbo of CVs and the sort of queues I left Ireland to avoid twenty-five years ago.

He rises and walks stage left.

My only routine is spending two hours every afternoon sitting with my mother, who stubbornly clings to her home, complaining about the care-workers who come in three times a day like she was some sort of patient. Conversation with her is hard and so is finding a parking space on her road. I drop Dieter off at her door and park on a double yellow line three streets away. (*Calls*) Dieter, where are you?

(*As Dieter*) I'm up here. I don't think her care-worker came this morning: I think she's been lying on the landing all night.

(*Own voice*) A coat over her nightgown, her good hat on as if going to meet someone off a train. She lasts for two days in intensive care, fighting for each breath. Dieter in tears in the hospital corridor, texting his girlfriend: it's her arms he wants. I watch them embrace when she arrives, sensing two generations slip away from me.

Moves upstage.

(*To audience*) I only ever beat Dieter at chess once, when he was twelve. He's always been three moves ahead of me ever since: even today in Paris where, amid an onslaught of green jerseys and hats and plastic hammers, we board a metro for the Stade de France. With just Dieter and me it would be a wake. With just Shane and me we'd run out of things to say, but with Shane and Dieter and me it works somehow. The carriage throbs with song.

(*As Shane, sings*)
As she wheels her wheelbarrow,
Through streets broad and narrow, crying:
Ireland! Ireland!

(*As Dieter*) Is there any way you could all agree on the one key? Dieter asks.

(*As Shane*) There are three great lies, Shane tells him: I'll only put it in a little bit, Stephen Ireland's granny is dead and the Irish can sing in tune.

Moves forward.

(*To audience*) Theo thinks there is a fourth great lie. He keeps telling me at Ma's funeral that all this talk of a property bust is an unpatriotic saboteur's lie invented by newspaper columnists. The doomsayers invent it so well that Ma's house doesn't get one bidder, even when we drop the price by forty percent. Meanwhile the shares I hold for Dieter's future plummet every time I turn on a radio. Then I wake one morning to find that Anglo Irish Bank – whose shares have dropped to just two percent of their old value – is nationalised. The bank is worthless, a crock of pure shite. Dieter's inheritance is gone. I've fucked up, fucked up. I go into the kitchen where he is studying. It doesn't seem long since he would drag me from bed in Hamburg so he could draw perfect houses.

He was always going to be an architect. If he's going to be an architect he will have to live elsewhere. Dieter looks up.

(*As Dieter*) Let's not talk about it now, Dad; I've exams in two months time. Let's talk about it then.

He sits on centre seats.

(*To audience*) The week of his exams I take a last spin on the motorbike, trying to locate the spot where Dublin's new houses finally stop. Ghost estates half built, cement mixers abandoned, exposed rafters left to rot in the rain. I park on a flood plain and I could be anywhere or nowhere. Here and there an isolated light where someone purchased at the height of the boom. These are the estates the Poles were rushing to build where they ploughed into Frieda. Two nights later a youth answers my ad about selling the motorbike. He pays in cash with barely a glance at the bike. After he drives it off I realise he is simply laundering drugs cash.

When I miss my first mortgage repayment my bank manager starts to phone daily. I have him by day and the people who have moved in above me by night. I don't know what language they speak, there's just a thump, thump of rap music as Dieter studies with his headphones on and I sit up drinking cheap wine and obsessing about money. I've fucked up. I let myself believe in the country that fucked up my father, that shipped off my uncles and aunts like cattle on the hoof.

Stands.

(*As Dieter*) Just fucking stop it, Dieter says. I can hear your brain wheeling. Stop beating yourself up. I never wanted the blood money from Mutti's death, I simply want her.

(*Own voice*) The money was for your future, son.

(*As Dieter*) My future doesn't belong to you or to Ireland either. You Irish are so desperate to belong and yet desperate to escape. I don't need to belong anywhere.

(*To audience*) Dieter rarely speaks so sharply but it's something that needs to be said: a declaration of independence, expressed just weeks before we celebrate the first degree in my family – Dieter's graduation as a Bachelor of Architectural Science. I want Frieda to be at the graduation and my mother and father who left school at fourteen. Dieter's friends are celebrating in the D2 nightclub later, but Dieter and I go for a meal together first. After two more years you'll have your master's degree, I say.

He sits.

(*As Dieter*) I was thinking I might take a year off, he says, then maybe do my master's elsewhere. The truth is there won't be too many jobs in Ireland.

(*Own voice*) Where are you thinking of heading, son?

(*As Dieter*) I've been accepted for a one year working visa in Canada. Maybe I can manage to stay there and study. I need to spread my wings. There's nothing for me in Ireland except you. I need to see if I can make it on my own.

(*Own voice*) You'll make it anywhere, I say. In Canada the houses are so big they need architects to draw maps just so that people can find the bathroom. Parts of it are like Westmeath with snow, but they've no gobshites – all the gobshites get rounded up and deported to Alaska. It breaks my heart to see you go, but leaving Ireland may be the best thing you'll ever do.

(*As Dieter*) Leaving Ireland is easy, Dieter says. The hard bit is leaving you.

(*Own voice*) Don't worry about me, I say, I'll be fine.

(*As Dieter*) Dad, you're starting to sound exactly like your mother.

(*Own voice*) You still have a few bob coming to you, I say. Not all the shares were in Anglo Irish. The others have plummeted too, but there's still a couple of thousand Euro if you cash them in. It will pay for your flight.

(*As Dieter*) Flights, he says.

(*Own voice*) There's more than one?

(*As Dieter*) On November 18th I fly to Canada, but only after you and me fly to Paris first for the World Cup playoff second leg. Think I'd let you bite your nails through that alone? I've already bought three tickets.

(*Own voice*) Why do we need three tickets? I ask. Besides you can't blow what little money you have like that.

(*As Dieter*) It's my money, Dad. I need you to do two things for me.

(*Own voice*) What?

(*As Dieter*) There's an urn taking up space on our hall table. You keep promising to phone Shane.

(*Own voice*) Shane is my oldest friend, I say. That means I barely know what to say to him anymore.

(*As Dieter*) Tell him there's a match ticket waiting for him at Charles de Gaulle airport. And if you've nothing to say to old friends, maybe you need to make some new ones. That's the second thing I need you to do: fill out a form.

(*Own voice*) I spend my days filling out forms. My CV is the only thing keeping that photocopying shop around the corner going.

(*As Dieter*) I mean a different type of form, Dad. Life isn't all about jobs. You're not the first unemployed person and you won't be the last. Fill out the form on this website.

He stands.

(*Own voice*) Wait a second, I say, looking at the website address he hands me. This is an online dating agency. You're not serious.

(*As Dieter*) I'm deadly serious. It's called starting to live again.

(*Own voice*) I'm not sticking up personal information on the web for the whole world – including my own son – to read.

(*As Dieter*) Welcome to the twenty-first century, Dad.

(*Own voice*) Call me old fashioned, I say, but I prefer virtually no sex to virtual sex.

(*As Dieter*) Can't you see, Dad? You're going to trap me with the same guilt that brought you back to Ireland because of your mother. I want to be bound by love and not guilt. I blamed you for Mutti's death. She came here for your sake. I resented you and I felt guilty for resenting you. I was so desperate to mind you that I've never asked you for anything, but I'm asking you now to fill in that form.

(*To Audience*) Feck it, when he says it like that I can hardly refuse. Dieter goes off to join his fellow graduates in the nightclub and I go home to the negative equity apartment we won't share for much longer. He's right to go. If I were his age I'd go. But I feel how Ma must have felt the night I told her I had a ticket booked for Germany. Then, because I don't want to think any more, I click on the website Dieter mentioned. I pay my subscription and fill in the form. A different type of CV: an audition for a different life. I refuse to lie or exaggerate. I admit to being lonely, to feeling spent, but I also know I have a lot to give because I've known love in my life. I fill out the form like a pessimist who believes in miracles and because Dieter does not come home that night, because he's breaking up with his girlfriend, setting himself free of all ties, I sit up peering into other people's lives. In the following days I send out uncertain, tentative messages. Some replies are fake, some scary, but I also find people who want to talk, who are also starting out again, rebuilding stalled lives. I am in no hurry to meet anyone and the first few times I do – for awkward coffees in town – I'm in no hurry to meet them again. But it's new and intriguing and each time I shave to meet someone Dieter stands in the bathroom doorway fussing so much that I laugh and tell him to feck off. We're like brothers really as November 18th creeps closer, with every day special because it's one day closer to when we won't be together.

(*As Dieter*) I fly to Canada from Paris, Dieter says, and you fly back to Ireland. It means neither of us have to wave the other off or leave the other behind. We're both starting new journeys, Dad.

(*To audience*) My new friend Laima thinks he's wise. She's not really my friend because I've only met her four times, but I like her, we're comfortable together. At first we were each afraid that the other was dying to jump into bed. In Latvian Laima means luck. She's not a bit like Frieda, but maybe one day we'll feel close enough for me to discover that she also smells warm and sexy and vaguely Lutheran. She has a son of fourteen and an ex-husband I don't know much about. She has a job in Dunne's stores which is more than I have. I don't know many Latvian words yet, but Laima apparently means luck.

He moves back to stand in front of the centre seats.

Ireland could have used some luck in the Stade de France tonight. Shane and Dieter and me squeeze in among the Irish fans. We may be broke and scarred as a nation, but once the game starts we forget everything as we sing our hearts out for the lads. For ninety minutes I can even set aside the fact that my son is about to emigrate, because every primeval instinct from my boyhood is kicking in. I'm a six-year-old boy in a pub again with Da and Ma listening to Ireland lose forty-four years ago. I'm a teenager in Dalymount cascading down the terrace in an ecstatic crowd when Don Givens scores a hat-trick against Russia. I'm a young immigrant standing with Shane and Mick and the Irish crowd at Stuttgart. I do not know what the future holds. I just know that I am happy to stand with my oldest friend and my beloved son; to stand among people who have travelled from Ireland and Irish people who found their way here from every corner of Europe.

We lost the first leg in Dublin to a fluky, deflected goal on a night when we played timidly as if too scared to believe in ourselves. But from the opening whistle in Paris we can see that this Irish team believe in each other and would kill for each other and we begin to believe in ourselves too. (*Calls*) Ireland, Ireland. (*Takes off his jumper and stands up on the central seats*) Who says that we're out on our feet? Maybe we're up against the wall, but it's like we've found a new bedrock here. We may be broken-hearted in ninety minutes time, but what's the point in being alive if you're afraid to have your heart broken? And in the Stade de France I remember what it feels like to be alive.

They can keep Zinedine Zidane, because out on the pitch we have Zinedine Kilbane, almost as old as myself, but with an honest heart that will try forever. After thirty-three minutes he sets up Duff to lay it back for Robbie Keane to score. My arms are around Dieter with Shane screaming on top of us. Every farmyard animal with a face like Mick McCarthy's starts to get nervous again. The tie is level, balanced on a knife edge. Lawrence and Doyle are chasing everything. The second half kicks off and O'Shea blasts over the bar. It's all Ireland. Duff forces a crucial save from their keeper, then Keane darts through and rounds everybody, including the post.

(*As Shane*) Holy Jesus, my heart isn't able for this, Shane says. Move over in that fucking urn, Mick.

(*Own voice*) We're going to do it, I tell him; we're going to win.

(*As Shane*) Fucking right we are. Come on, Robbie Keane, give us a second belter, Shane shouts, I haven't had two orgasms in the same hour since 1995.

(*Own voice*) We're not fucked as a nation tonight – we're walking tall. Unemployed women in Sligo and bankrupt builders, too fat to squeeze through their windows and jump off penthouse balconies, are screaming as one. (*Calls*) Ireland.

Then, with eight minutes left, there's a free kick into the Irish box. Paul McShane watches the ball float out of play. But Thierry Henry is there to stretch out his hand for two illicit flicks of his wrist – one to stop the ball crossing the by-line, the second to tee it up for a flick across the box for Gallas to score. I can see him cheat, Dieter can see him, astronauts in the space station are screaming at their monitors, but the Swedish referee has a blindness gleaned from generations of self-abuse. Shay Given pleads with him, devastated, while the French celebrate.

(*As Shane*) Cheating bastards, Shane says. They promised to help the rebels in Wexford in 1798 and what did the fuckers do only turn up two months too fucking late in fucking Mayo?

(*As Dieter*) That was two hundred and eleven years ago, Dieter says.

(*As Shane*) And I was just getting over it when that bastard Henry did this.

(*As Dieter*) You're right, Dieter says. Bastards.

(*Own voice*) I didn't know you really cared, I tell Dieter.

(*Dieter's voice*) Neither did I (*Shouts*) Scheissfranzose!

(*Own voice*) He's telling Henry he's a cheating bastard, I explain to an old Dub standing behind us.

(*Dublin accent*) He took the words right outta me mouth.

He gets down off the seats.

(*To audience*) Then we can't hear ourselves talk any more because the Irish crowd are shouting our team forward for one last push. There's no barriers here now, no millionaires on that pitch, just eleven Irishmen sharing the same dream as us. The clock ticks down, with Dieter as passionate as Shane, my son about to follow him into exile. I'm screaming for Ireland, yet I'm also trying savour these moments together, united by a common dream. We're in the dying seconds, with a last free hit too long to the back post. The referee blows. Shay Given falls to his knees; Duff is in tears. As Richard Dunne sits quietly on the turf, Thierry Henry sidles up to sit quietly beside him, like a semi-apologetic thief.

He sits on the actual stage.

(*As Shane*) At least he has the grace to apologise, Shane says quietly. Unlike some.

(*To audience*) He's thinking of the same folk I am – those who cheated us blind for a decade – bankers and developers and politicians and every two-bit huckster with an inflated ego who played on our fears that our children would get left behind. They're not sitting out on that turf, they're apologising to no one. It's not Thierry Henry who is putting my child on an aeroplane tonight.

I won't be thinking of him when I'm standing in a queue hoping to get an interview for some temporary Christmas job. I'm angry but I have bigger fish to fry. (*Puts jumper back on*) Dieter and I don't join in the chants of "cheat, cheat, cheat", though we join the applause as each shattered Irish player gives his shirt and his boots to the crowd. C'mon Dieter, I say, you have a plane to catch. Let's go, son, I say, as the players enter the tunnel and the stewards turn away.

(*As Dieter, running to seats, stage right*) Fuck the Champs-Élysées, Dieter says and puts one foot over the advertising hoarding. This is where we leave him.

(*To Dieter*) What are you doing, son?

(*As Dieter, standing up on the seats*) If Thierry Henry can bend the rules so can we.

(*To audience*) Dieter grins and it's exactly my dead father's grin. It's the grin I had at his age, before I started always worrying about the consequences. He hands me the urn from the bag at my feet.

(*As Dieter*) Let's do this, he says. You two fossils need the exercise.

He jumps down onto far side of seats.

(*To audience*) He hops over the hoarding and I find myself chasing after him onto the turf of the Stade de France. (*Calls*) Dieter, you'll get us all arrested.

(*As Shane*) Please God they'll give me a lifetime ban, says Shane suddenly, panting alongside me like he used to chase down the wing in Fairview Park. Wouldn't it be great not to have to go through this torment every four years?

(*To audience*) Ahead of us, Dieter turns.

(*As Dieter*) Come on, scatter the ashes quick.

(*Shane's voice*) Not in the bleeding goalmouth, we won't, Shane shouts. Mick hated being stuck in goals. He was our midfield general.

(*As Dieter*) Will you make up your mind then? Before Asterix and Obelix hobble us.

(*To audience*) Dieter was right. Four French stewards are heading towards us: weightlifters recently banned for steroid abuse. Dieter blocks them off. For a lad who only plays table tennis he's doing well. As two of them grapple with him, Shane distracts the other two with a version of the New Zealand Haka known only in Cabra. But a have-a-go-hero in an FAI blazer decides to join in. It's only a question of whether he'll flatten me or have a heart attack first. I want to hit the little jumped up official, but he stops and says:

(*Dublin accent*) Jaysus, Eoin is it? And Shane? I remember him doing those same dance steps with my sister in Zhivago's.

(*Own voice*) His face comes back from years ago when he had a mop of untidy brown hair and we used to meet at Bohs games in Dalymount. Dudley, I say, because that was our nickname for him. He grins.

(*As Dudley*) It's years since anyone called me Dudley.

(*To audience*) Then he flattens me, and Mick – or whatever remains of Mick – slips from my grasp. A fourteen-stone Bohs fan lies on top of me covered in ashes.

(*As Dudley*) That's not cocaine, he asks.

(*As Shane*) It is in my bollix, Shane says, being throttled by a steward. That's Mick McKenna. You remember Mick?

(*As Dudley*) I just wouldn't recognise him without the waistcoat, Dudley says. Isn't it amazing what the years can do to you?

(*To audience*) Suddenly men with walkie-talkies and flak jackets and a congestion of policemen and fellows who could be lawyers from the European Court of Justice are standing over us: more people than Athlone Town get for home matches. (*Moves upstage*) Everyone wants a piece of me: I'm like Eircom being floated during the boom. Dudley keeps telling them to go easy in his best Stonybatter French and I'm telling them to leave Dieter alone because he's a conscientious objector to nationalism and sport.

He moves to the space beyond the stage left seats.

Mick's ashes are being trampled into the turf as we're carried into the tunnel where an ashen faced Robbie Keane is about to do an interview. He's smaller in real life, especially when you're being carried upside-down. Giovanni Trapattoni shakes his head sadly, dressed like a Crumlin chip shop owner at a wedding, and Robbie Keane, amid his heartache, tells the security men to go easy, lads. Dudley joins in, starting to distract the French security men by arguing with them. Borrowing a trick from Robbie Keane, he points one finger behind his back in the direction he wants us to go. Shane sees it and joins in too. I take the hint. Missed flights to Ireland or Holland are not the end of the world, but Canada is a long way away.

He moves along the space behind the centre seats.

As discrete as a man can be when covered in ash, I steer Dieter past the angry press briefings in the tunnel, following the signs that say Sortie. I'm waiting for a hand on my shoulder and for handcuffs, but we find our way out onto the concourse where crowds hurry away.

He moves centre stage.

(*To Dieter*) We could have ended up in a police cell, I tell Dieter. I'd swear you don't want to get on that plane.

(As Dieter) What are my other options?

(Own Voice) You could try Hamburg.

(*As Dieter)* Someone did that before me. I want a blank canvas, a fresh start. Tell me you'll be okay.

(*Own voice*) I'll be fine. You can't live my life for me any more than I can live yours for you, son.

(*To audience*) We stand in silence on the packed platform of Le Plaine Stade de France. And we don't say much when the train to the airport comes. We fight our way on board and head for

Charles de Gaulle. It was all train stations once, my scenes of homecomings and reunions. It's airports now and bottled water slightly cheaper than uranium. Dieter has planned it well: I'm not seeing him off because we're both departing on different flights. We stop at an escalator, like the one in Westland Row where I held my father's hand forty-four years ago. I look at Dieter's shoulder bag. You're not taking much, I say.

(*As Dieter*) I'm taking a lot, Dieter says. In here (*Points to his head and then his heart*) and in here.

(*Own voice*) Your mother loved you very much. You know that, don't you?

(*As Dieter*) I know Dad.

(*Own voice*) And I love you very much.

(*As Dieter*) I love you too, Dad.

(*Own voice*) That makes me rich beyond measure.

(*As Dieter*) Rich and with a hot date with Laima when you go home tonight.

(*Own voice*) I mightn't call in, I'm a bit nervous.

(*As Dieter*) Call to her, Dad. Tell her your two jokes: you've told them to everybody else. It is a pity we didn't win tonight, we came so close.

(*Own voice, softly*) There'll be other playoffs, son, just you wait and see.

(*To audience*) Then we do something we've never done. But it seems fitting, like at the end of a match. We shake hands. Before he can embrace me I walk away and I don't look back. Something about him would remind me too much of Frieda or too much of myself and I want to set him free.

He sits on the centre seats and, taking his scarf from his bag, he puts it on.

I don't know what happened to Shane. I brush whatever ash I can off my clothes and catch the last flight to Dublin. Here I am now in this airport. Time to quit stalling and join the queue for late night taxies, the Irish fans nursing grievances like heirlooms, the backpackers and migrant workers. I'm coming home alone, but maybe I won't always be alone. Call in, Laima says in her text, no matter how late. I have been loved and been hurt. I need to open myself up to the risks of being hurt or being loved again. It's time to enter my native city like a foreigner. Because Dublin isn't mine: it's a million stories deep, a million lives being lived in Santry and Whitehall, Drumcondra and Dorset Street, along the quays to the Liberties and Christchurch, all the way to the artisan cottage, where Laima is waiting with a bottle of wine and a meal kept hot.

He hums distractedly as he picks up his shoulder bag.

Alive-alive-o!

Alive-alive-o!

Stephen Ireland's two grannies

Are…

(*To audience*) Everyone is so busy in airports that nobody has time to figure out what I've been waiting for. I've been waiting for the rest of my life to catch up. It's only half time in it, with extra time to come. (*Starts to exit*) Blow your whistle, ref: let the rest of my life begin.

He exits. Lights down.